EXPLORING CI

THE MOVEMENT
1963

ANGELA SHANTÉ

Franklin Watts®
An imprint of Scholastic Inc.

Content Consultants

Senator Nan Grogan Orrock
State of Georgia

Crystal R. Sanders, Ph.D.
Associate Professor of History
Pennsylvania State University

Library of Congress Cataloging-in-Publication Data
Names: Shanté, Angela, author.
Title: Exploring civil rights— the movement : 1963 / by Angela Shanté.
Description: First edition. | New York : Franklin Watts, an imprint of Scholastic Inc., [2022] | Series:
   Exploring civil rights | Includes bibliographical references and index. | Audience: Ages 10–14. |
   Audience: Grades 5–8.
Identifiers: LCCN 2021020379 (print) | LCCN 2021020380 (ebook) | ISBN 9781338769807 (library
   binding) | ISBN 9781338769814 (paperback) | ISBN 9781338769821 (ebook)
Subjects: LCSH: African Americans—Civil rights—History—Juvenile literature. | Civil rights
   movements—United States—History—20th century—Juvenile literature. | Civil rights
   workers—United States—Juvenile literature. | BISAC: JUVENILE NONFICTION / History /
   United States / 20th Century | JUVENILE NONFICTION / History / United States / General
Classification: LCC E185.61 .S525 2022 (print) | LCC E185.61 (ebook) | DDC 323.1196/073—dc23
LC record available at https://lccn.loc.gov/2021020379
LC ebook record available at https://lccn.loc.gov/2021020380

10 9 8 7 6 5 4 3 2 1   22 23 24 25 26

Printed in Heshan, China 62
First edition, 2022

ON THE COVER: The Reverend Dr. Martin Luther King, Jr. giving his "I Have a Dream" speech to a crowd of 250,000 at the March on Washington on August 28, 1963.

Series produced by 22MediaWorks, Inc.
President LARY ROSENBLATT
Book design by FABIA WARGIN and AMELIA LEON
Editor SUSAN ELKIN
Copy Editor LAURIE LIEB
Fact Checker BRETTE SEMBER
Photo Researcher DAVID PAUL PRODUCTIONS

PREVIOUS PAGE: Demonstrators picket in front of a school board office protesting segregation of students.

The Children's Crusade, page 30

Table of Contents

Medgar Evers, page 51

Black and white citizens at a barbecue on an Alabama plantation are separated by a wall in 1935.

The Way It Was

In December 1865, the Thirteenth Amendment to the U.S. Constitution abolished slavery in the United States. By the early 1870s, former slaveholding states in the South created Black codes to strictly limit the freedom of their Black citizens. These restrictions were known as **"Jim Crow"** laws, and they controlled where people who used to be enslaved could live and work.

Jim Crow laws were expanded in the 1880s to keep Black citizens from voting or receiving a proper education. In many parts of the South, they were forced to use separate restaurants, schools, restrooms, parks, and other public places. This practice is known as **segregation**. Although laws said that these spaces should be "separate but equal," facilities for Black people were almost always inferior to those assigned to white citizens.

It was not uncommon for Black citizens in the South to be kidnapped and beaten, shot, or killed for small violations of Jim Crow laws. **Lynchings** and white mob violence frequently terrorized many Black communities. Black churches were burned down, and Black homes attacked. **Discrimination** against Black Americans also existed in the North and elsewhere in the nation, but less so than in the South at the time.

Fighting Back

Segregation, Jim Crow laws, and discrimination denied Black Americans the same **civil rights** as white Americans. In the face of **oppression** and terror, some Black Americans organized to fight inequality. The first civil rights organization in the United States was founded in 1896 as the National Association of Colored Women's Clubs. In 1909, an interracial group of **activists** formed the National Association for the Advancement of Colored People (NAACP). The NAACP called for an end to segregation in schools, public transportation, and other areas of daily life. The group also focused on making the American public aware of the violence against Black people.

In the following years, new civil rights groups emerged. Christian ministers, African American lawyers, and Black youth were especially important in organizing and supporting the emerging civil rights movement. The decade between 1955 and 1965 would serve as the heart of the movement, as action and long awaited progress began to take shape.

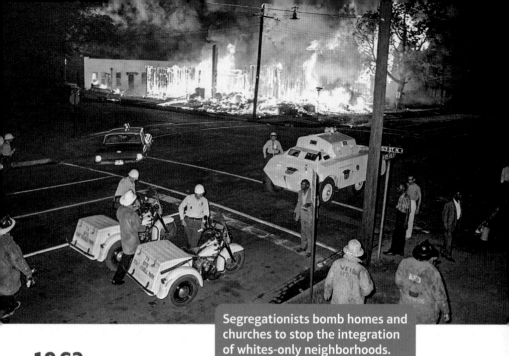

Segregationists bomb homes and churches to stop the integration of whites-only neighborhoods.

1963

This book shows how the progress made throughout 1963 was tempered by the violence surrounding it. The year began with a focus on Alabama and the effort to change the discriminatory laws that kept Black Americans from enjoying public spaces and equal employment opportunities. A change in strategy by civil rights leaders in April would bring children to the movement, testing the commitment of the entire Black community in Birmingham. The March on Washington in August took the battle for equality to Washington, DC, pushing Congress further toward legislation. The planning involved in these and other campaigns for justice during 1963 would prove to be a critical turning point in the civil rights movement nationwide. ■

During the course of the civil rights movement of 1963, President John F. Kennedy delivered several speeches advocating for peace and nonviolence.

A Turbulent Start to the Year

By 1963, the civil rights movement in the United States was entering a **volatile** phase. Some white Americans fought hard to keep Black citizens from achieving the freedom to vote, to use public spaces, and to shop, live, and work where they wanted. Although this pushback was widespread across the country, the loudest objections were still coming from the South.

The Fight Shifts to Alabama

In 1963, the American Southeast was still one of the most segregated regions in the nation. Black residents in these states were some of the most oppressed in the nation. They lived in segregated neighborhoods, attended segregated schools, and used segregated facilities. **Amenities** that were designated for Blacks-only use in the South were poorly equipped, run-down, and underfunded compared to their white counterparts.

Some white residents of these states came from families that had once enslaved Black Americans. They held on to the same beliefs about race that their ancestors had. They didn't see the need to change their traditions regarding the separation of white and Black races. One of the loudest opponents of the civil rights movement in the South was Alabama's governor, George Wallace.

Support for Segregation

On January 14, 1963, George Wallace took office as the governor of Alabama. Prior to this election victory, Wallace, a Democrat, had suffered a humiliating defeat in a failed run for governor. He blamed his 1958 loss and his low polling numbers on his **moderate** views on segregation. After the loss, Wallace adopted a harder stance on segregation.

Governor George Wallace used his political power and position to intimidate civil rights leaders in hopes of hindering the movement.

By 1963, many segregation laws were deemed **unconstitutional**; however, southern states maintained the unofficial laws of Jim Crow.

During his 1962 campaign Wallace used every speaking engagement as an opportunity to emphasize his resistance to the civil rights movement. He promised that, if elected, he would fight to keep Jim Crow laws in place in Alabama. Thanks to this position, Wallace won the governor's seat. At his inauguration, Wallace spoke to his white base of supporters, promising "segregation now . . . segregation tomorrow . . . segregation forever."

The Emancipation Proclamation

On January 1, 1863, President Abraham Lincoln signed the Emancipation Proclamation into law. Many believe that this was the law that abolished slavery. However, Lincoln's proclamation applied only to those states that had seceded from the Union. The new law declared that "all persons held as slaves within any States, or designated part of the State, the people whereof shall be in rebellion against the United States, shall be then, thenceforward, and forever free." However, those rebellious states did not believe they were subject to Lincoln's order. As a result of their defiance, the Emancipation Proclamation directly linked the Civil War to slavery.

Abraham Lincoln was the 16th president of the United States.

Lincoln hoped that the Emancipation Proclamation would end the Civil War by weakening the economy of the southern states. He believed that newly freed people would move away from the South, leaving those states without the free labor they needed to run their farms and businesses. The president thought the North could then easily defeat the South and preserve the Union. However, enslaved people in states that were loyal to the Union would have to wait two more years before they would be freed.

The Emancipation Proclamation also allowed Black soldiers to fight for the Union army. As the war continued, many African Americans in the South fled to Union army camps to escape bondage. Some ended up fighting alongside white soldiers. Other slaves were killed trying to flee their captors. And many African Americans who stayed on their plantations remained enslaved and were forced to continue working without pay, and living under horrible conditions, despite the law of the land.

The Civil War ended on April 9, 1865, when the southern states that had seceded surrendered to the Union Army. The conflict claimed the lives of more than 600,000 soldiers. On December 6, the Thirteenth Amendment freeing all enslaved people in the United States was ratified.

Freed slaves gather on the banks of a canal in Richmond, Virginia, in 1865.

Arthur Shores was a civil rights activist and lawyer who worked to integrate segregated schools and higher educational institutions.

All Eyes on Birmingham

Many government officials in Alabama strongly believed in segregation. In the 1940s, local Black activist Arthur Shores filed a **lawsuit** against Birmingham's segregated **zoning** law, which denied African American families entry into whites-only neighborhoods. Shores wanted Black residents to have the freedom to purchase homes in any neighborhood they might choose. A judge eventually ruled that the segregated zoning law was unconstitutional. After this win, Samuel Matthews became the first African American in Birmingham to purchase a home in the whites-only neighborhood of Smithsfield. This victory was short-lived, however. On the first day the Matthews family was to move in, their home was bombed and destroyed.

In the 1950s, the right to vote and the **integration** of schools took center stage in Birmingham. Local organizers like the NAACP attempted to integrate schools like the University of Alabama, but were denied. Despite the ruling in *Brown v. Board of Education of Topeka* that prohibited segregation in schools, Birmingham schools remained segregated. Similarly, Black residents of Birmingham were

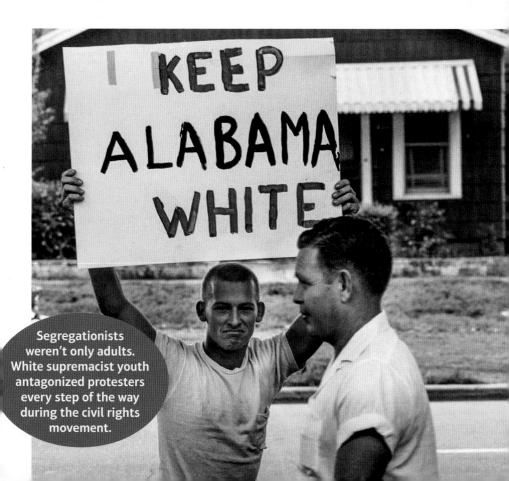

Segregationists weren't only adults. White supremacist youth antagonized protesters every step of the way during the civil rights movement.

consistently denied the right to vote. Organizations like the Southern Negro Youth Conference conducted protests and marches to make state officials abide by the law. But most attempts to register African American voters in the state were met with violence and various legal schemes. A **poll tax** was enacted in many areas, requiring citizens to pay a fee in order to vote. The price tag was out of reach for many African Americans at the time. Another obstacle was the imposed "**literacy** test" for Black voters. This forced Black citizens to pass a lengthy 30-question quiz in 10 minutes. If they did not pass the quiz, they were disqualified and could not vote.

Elected officials of the South shouting their opposition to proposed civil rights reforms at the Democratic National Convention.

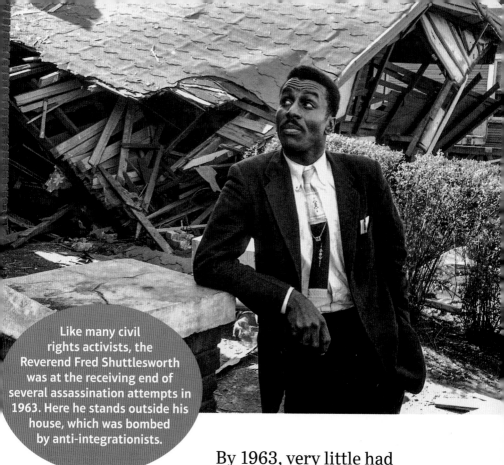

Like many civil rights activists, the Reverend Fred Shuttlesworth was at the receiving end of several assassination attempts in 1963. Here he stands outside his house, which was bombed by anti-integrationists.

By 1963, very little had changed for African American residents in Birmingham. Many civil rights activists, including the Reverend Dr. Martin Luther King, Jr., called the city "the most segregated city in America." Local activists from the Alabama Christian Movement for Human Rights (ACMHR), led by Fred Shuttlesworth, were at a standstill with local officials who refused to budge on any civil rights demands. One of the biggest roadblocks was Theophilus Eugene "Bull" Connor, who served as the commissioner of public safety, governing both the police and fire departments of Birmingham.

With the support of newly installed governor George Wallace, the city council enacted a segregation **ordinance** in Birmingham. This ordinance called for the "separation of races," a decision that placed local state law above the **federal** courts that had required the integration of public spaces like schools and parks. Instead of adhering to federal court rulings, this local Birmingham ordinance gave Connor the power to close public spaces instead of desegregating them. At the start of 1963, more than 60 public parks in Birmingham had been closed in opposition to integration.

Commissioner Bull Connor (center) was adamantly against the civil rights movement. He used his power and control over the police and fire departments to detain civil rights protestors.

Dr. King Is Invited to Birmingham

Civil rights leaders decided to increase their pressure for the city of Birmingham to obey federal laws. Shuttlesworth invited Dr. King to join the efforts in Alabama. Shuttlesworth hoped that a team composed of King, president of the Southern Christian Leadership Conference (SCLC), and Reverend James Bevel, its director of Direct Action and Nonviolent Education in Montgomery, along with ACMHR could replicate some of the success of the bus **boycott**. In 1956, the city of Montgomery, Alabama, had **desegregated** city buses after a yearlong boycott by its Black citizens.

Dr. King (bottom left) and other civil rights leaders attempted to work with Birmingham electe officials to construct a desegregation plan.

Accepting the invitation, the SCLC arrived in Birmingham in April. Alongside the ACMHR, they launched the Birmingham Campaign. The campaign was planned to start on April 3, 1963.

The Birmingham Campaign

The Birmingham Campaign consisted of three main areas of focus. The first goal was to desegregate the stores in the downtown area of the city. Civil rights activists wanted Black patrons who spent their money in these stores to be able to use the front door, rather than a Blacks-only entrance, and to shop without **scrutiny**. Another goal during the campaign was to shed light on the unfair employ-ment policies within the state.

Fred Shuttlesworth

Fred Shuttlesworth was a minister who helped found the ACMHR and the SCLC. He helped plan strategy for the major events of the movement and was the target of violence on many occasions. Unlike King's, Shuttlesworth's approach was usually blunt and direct. He created plans for the Birmingham Campaign that were known as Project "C" for confrontation. While he worked within the organization, he and King often disagreed about the direction of the movement and their decision to choose nonviolence. In 2001, President Bill Clinton awarded Shuttlesworth the Presidential Citizens Medal.

Fred Shuttlesworth, cofounder of the Southern Christian Leadership Conference, was a leading voice in the civil rights movement.

During the Birmingham Campaign, several nonviolent protests, like this march on city hall, were planned.

The SCLC wanted to ensure that Black employees were afforded the same employment opportunities as white workers in the state. The third goal of the campaign targeted the closure of parks and other public spaces. The ACMHR and SCLC planned a series of **sit-ins**, marches, protests, and boycotts to highlight each of these areas.

Both organizations trained participants to follow the ways of nonviolent protest and to ensure that each protest obeyed the laws of the state. The city of Birmingham had enacted a new **injunction** prohibiting activists from picketing, demonstrating, protesting, or parading in Birmingham without a permit. Local officials, who were admittedly against integration and the civil rights movement, hoped that these new laws would deter activists. But they were wrong.

Civil rights activists saw these laws for what they were: attempts to silence their demands. In a unanimous decision, civil rights leaders decided to ignore the injunctions. Instead, Shuttlesworth and King pressed forward with a planned march scheduled for April 12. On that day the procession heading toward city hall was met with police blockades and warnings to leave. Refusing the order, more than 50 protesters, including King, were arrested. Each activist was charged with **contempt of court** and parading without a permit. Bail was set at $1,500, which was much higher than the standard $200 bail for similar offenses by white citizens. This higher fine, like many of the state laws in Alabama, was an attempt to silence the movement.

A Black man is detained by police as protesters march toward city hall on April 12, 1963.

King was immediately separated from the other protesters and placed alone in a cell, where he was denied visitors or calls. He would spend more than a week in a jail cell by himself. During that week, a friend managed to get a newspaper to King. The Birmingham paper carried an open letter written in response to the protest by eight white Christian ministers. They openly questioned King's methods, his timing, and why his focus was on their state.

The Reverend Ralph Abernathy and Dr. King (right) were arrested several times for organizing and leading the civil rights movement.

Dr. King used his time in jail to spotlight injustices in the country.

King was offended by the letter and on April 16 began drafting a response in the margins of the newspaper. King wrote, "I am in Birmingham because injustice is here." He continued by explaining his methods, timing, and focus on Birmingham. Passionately, he declared, "justice too long delayed is justice denied." King's letter was smuggled out of the jail and copied and distributed throughout the community. It was published in pamphlet form and appeared in several magazines, becoming widely known as the Letter from Birmingham Jail. ▪

Dr. King's wife, Coretta Scott King, speaks with President Kennedy by phone on April 15, 1963, regarding racial tensions in Birmingham, where her husband is in jail.

2

The Children Will Lead the Way

While Dr. King and the other protesters were detained in prison, civil rights organizations worked to raise funds to get them released from jail. The efforts were an uphill battle as money and participation started to dwindle. Nevertheless, civil rights attorneys and organizations were able to free most participants on that same day.

Still in solitary confinement, King remained in jail. Increasingly worried about her husband's well-being, King's wife, Coretta, reached out to President Kennedy. Within a few days, Birmingham officials allowed Dr. King a phone call home. On April 20, King was finally released from jail.

After King's release, movement leaders held a meeting at the 16th Street Baptist Church to discuss the campaign. At the meeting, protesters

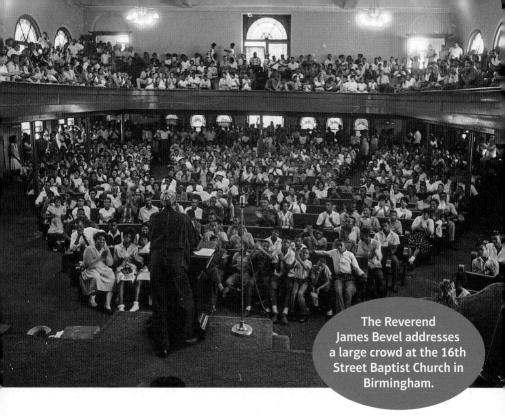

The Reverend James Bevel addresses a large crowd at the 16th Street Baptist Church in Birmingham.

expressed concern over their participation in the campaign. Many worried about losing their jobs or **endangering** their families. James Bevel suggested a radical idea. He proposed that the movement consider including children as young activists.

Although civil rights leaders (including King) were initially reluctant, they finally accepted Bevel's idea. The planned protest would be called the Children's Crusade. Organizers hoped that the protest would lead to a meeting with the mayor of Birmingham to discuss desegregating businesses, a request that had been repeatedly denied in the past. Thousands of young activists attended nonviolence workshops and were instructed on how to protest peacefully.

Mary Lucille Hamilton

Mary Lucille Hamilton was a civil rights activist who fought against injustices both large and small. As a field organizer for the Congress of Racial Equality (CORE), Hamilton participated in many protests, including one in Gadsden, Alabama, where she was arrested in April 1963. At a hearing later that spring, Hamilton refused to answer the judge until she was afforded the same courtesy as white people when being addressed: she wanted to be called "Miss Hamilton" instead of "Mary." Jailed for contempt of court, she was fined and remained locked up for five days. She appealed her conviction and with the NAACP's support, the case reached the U.S. Supreme Court, which ruled in her favor: Everyone is entitled to the same form of courteous address in a court of law, regardless of race.

Mary Lucille Hamilton

The Children's Crusade

On May 2, student activists walked out of schools all over Birmingham and gathered at the 16th Street Baptist Church. They then headed downtown to the business section of the city. Each student marched in a group until they arrived at their final destination. Some groups headed to city hall while others went to lunch counters to conduct sit-ins. The children sang songs, chanted, and marched with excitement. But as they made their way downtown, these feelings quickly changed.

As the children approached the business district, Commissioner Bull Connor and local officials met the procession with police barricades and warnings to leave.

Children as young as seven years old were detained, taken to jail, and fined for their participation in nonviolent protests.

Elected officials used increased bail amounts from youth activists as a means of bankrupting the movement.

Refusing to do so, more than 500 children were arrested and taken to jail in wagons and school buses waiting nearby. By the end of the day, city jails were filled to capacity so local officials used nearby fairgrounds to hold the Black protesters in police custody. On May 3, students again gathered in groups to march downtown. But, unlike the previous afternoon, Connor had a different plan. As the marchers approached the business area, they were met with police barricades once again. On this day, however, they were also met with violence. On Connor's orders, police officials attacked the young activists with fire hoses and police dogs. Students scattered to nearby parks and huddled in groups to provide shelter for one another.

As the civil rights movement gained steam and international attention, elected local officials pivoted to extreme measures such as the use of water cannons to deter protesters.

Hundreds of students were injured by fire hoses and bitten by police dogs. Many were jailed again.

Despite the horrendous treatment and possibility of being arrested, youth activists showed up every day, for four days, to participate in the movement. Media coverage of the crusade doubled after the second day of the march. Images from the crusade resulted in a national outcry and became a critical turning point in the movement. With all eyes on Birmingham, movement leaders now had the attention of the nation. And they would use the platform to advance their cause.

Loss of Profits

Local businesses were losing money during the protests. Stores remained closed during the crusade. Business owners feared that the bad press about their city would further hurt their companies. Hoping to de-escalate the situation themselves, merchants met with organizers to come up with a solution, but Shuttlesworth and King disagreed about the next move.

Shuttlesworth, who was in the hospital as a result of being injured by a fire hose, wanted to keep the pressure on. He thought the Children's Crusade was making the needed gains.

Police officers use police dogs to attack and disperse nonviolent protesters.

Three protesters join hands to help them withstand the force of powerful fire hoses.

King, on the other hand, wanted to meet business owners halfway by calling for all protests to stop. On May 10, King instructed the young activists to stop protesting, but he warned white business owners that the break might not last if the negotiations were not resolved quickly.

After two days of negotiation, a joint agreement was reached between the March organizers and Birmingham's businesses. The **truce**, called the Birmingham Agreement, was scheduled to begin within three days. It called for the removal of "Blacks-Only" and "Whites-Only" signs and the banning of segregated facilities within the business area. In addition to desegregating fitting rooms, lunch counters, and drinking fountains, store owners agreed to hire more Black salespeople and clerks. The hope was that the truce would stop the violence in the area, but it did not.

Short-Lived Victory

On May 11, the day after the Birmingham Agreement had been reached, residents of the city were shocked by a series of bombs. At 11 p.m., a passerby reported seeing a police car drop a package onto the porch of the home of Dr. King's younger brother, the Reverend A. D. Williams King, his wife, and five children. Another explosion occurred at the Gaston Motel, where Dr. King was staying. A bomb landed by the door to King's room and injured several people inside. No member of either King family was injured by the attacks. Many activists believed that members of the Birmingham police force and the **Ku Klux Klan** (KKK) were behind the bombings. Although investigated by the FBI, the bombings were never solved.

The Gaston Motel, where Dr. King was staying, when bombs ripped through the building.

A protester in Jackson, Mississippi, is dragged away by police during anti-segregation demonstrations on May 31, 1963.

Other Protests in May 1963

While the Birmingham Campaign was playing out, nonviolent protests were occurring in other regions of the South. Between May 18–21, students from CORE and the NAACP protested against segregated businesses and institutions in Durham, North Carolina. On May 22, thousands of protesters conducted a silent march in Greensboro, North Carolina, to highlight racial inequalities. During the months of May and June, activists in Jackson, Mississippi, organized a series of sit-ins and boycotts to challenge the unfair treatment of Black residents. At the same time, civil rights organizers in Danville, Virginia, were assaulted and jailed for supporting equal civil rights for Black residents.

Riots in the City

After the bombing at the Gaston Motel, Black citizens across Birmingham took to the streets. A small crowd gathered at both bombing locations. The destruction incited anger, frustration, and a sense of betrayal at the violence that continued despite the truce that was in place.

Crowds grew in size as the hours passed. Some people in the crowd sang spirituals like "We Shall Overcome"; others yelled for justice. Within the hour, squad cars and local officials arrived at the bomb sites. A. D. King stood on top of a car outside of his bombed house and asked the crowd to go home. Dr. King left for Atlanta as a safety precaution.

Some Black residents marched downtown while others stayed at the bomb sites and threw rocks at police officers. The protesters were again met with violence by local officials. Riots erupted within the 28 blocks surrounding the Gaston Motel. As early morning approached, so did state troopers with machine guns. Police officers viciously beat and arrested any Black person who was still in the area. The unrest continued into the early part of the following day. President Kennedy deployed the Alabama National Guard to restore order. ■

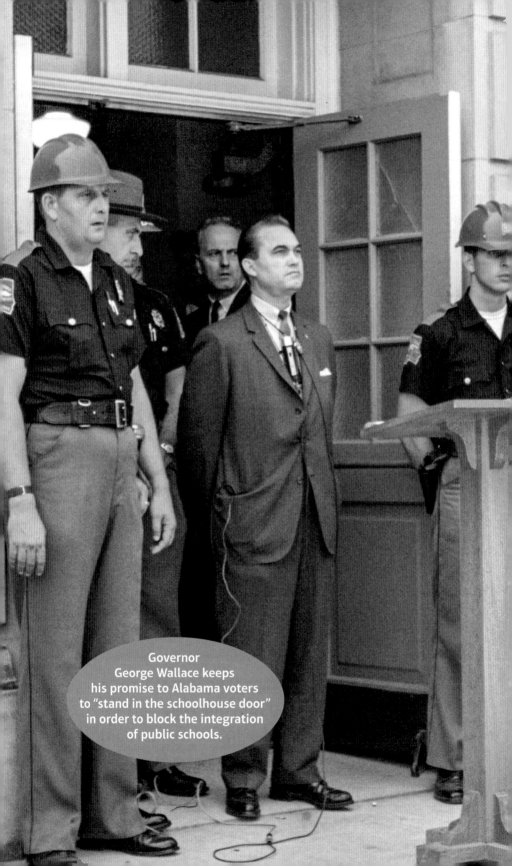

Governor George Wallace keeps his promise to Alabama voters to "stand in the schoolhouse door" in order to block the integration of public schools.

3

The Stand in the Schoolhouse Door

By June, civil rights leaders could see changes taking effect as a result of the Birmingham Campaign. Black residents in Birmingham had several reasons to celebrate: Jim Crow signs had been removed from local businesses, and Bull Connor, the public safety commissioner, was forced out of office. Seeing the gains as an opportunity to continue to fight for civil rights, movement leaders turned their focus to education.

From the Schoolhouse Door to the Supreme Court

Ever since all enslaved African Americans had been freed in 1865, their **descendants** had been fighting for equity within the education system. But by the mid-1900s, very little had changed.

Finally, in 1954, the Supreme Court unanimously ruled that segregated public schools were unconstitutional in the United States (*Brown v. Board of Education*). In 1955, a second case (*Brown v. Board of Education II*) ruled that schools should be integrated "with all deliberate speed." Another 1955 decision, *Lucy v. Adams*, stated that the University of Alabama had to admit all students, regardless of race.

Yet by 1963, very few schools across the country were following any of these federal laws. With legal support from organizations like the NAACP, civil rights activists filed educational lawsuits state by state to challenge the unconstitutional practices in public schools from primary school to universities.

White Americans picket with Black civil rights protesters in Trenton, New Jersey.

James Hood and
Vivian Malone

Planning for Integration

Vivian Malone was born on July 15, 1942, and graduated from her high school in Mobile, Alabama, in 1960. A member of the National Honor Society, Malone looked forward to going to college and making her parents proud. But, like many other Black students applying for higher education in 1963, her application to the University of Alabama was rejected.

James Hood, born on November 10, 1942, also wanted to attend the all-white University of Alabama. Hood, who was already attending Clark College in Atlanta, applied to the university to study clinical psychology, which was not offered at Clark.

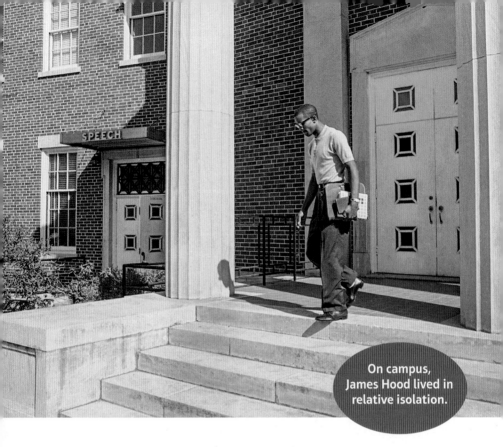

On campus, James Hood lived in relative isolation.

In support of Malone and Hood, the NAACP filed a lawsuit against the University of Alabama. But the two students weren't selected at random. They had undergone intensive vetting. Civil rights leaders across the country knew that the first Black students to integrate all-white institutions needed to be high academic achievers with spotless records. This meant they had to be ranked at the top of their class academically. Students also needed to have clean police records, which meant no prior arrests or any unlawful acts. Civil rights leaders didn't want to give school or law officials any cause to dismiss Black pupils. On May 16, 1963, a federal district court ruled in favor of the NAACP, permitting Hood and Malone to enroll at the university.

Civil rights organizations spent months counseling, advising, and planning the two students' entry into the university. Nothing was overlooked, not even their wardrobe. But despite the planning involved in preparing the Black students to integrate an all-white public institution, nothing could prepare them for the first day they stepped onto campus.

Vivian Malone was the only Black female student on campus at the University of Alabama in 1963.

Integration at the University of Alabama

Alabama governor George Wallace was also planning for the arrival of Hood and Malone. Since stepping into office in 1963, Wallace had made it known that he felt states' rights were more important than federal orders. He wanted to ensure that his state continued to remain segregated and that Alabama's Black residents never received civil rights equal to those enjoyed by the white residents of the state.

Malone and Hood were supposed to register for classes on June 11. As the day approached, Wallace expressed his determination to resist the integration of the university on TV and in local and national newspapers. On June 5, a federal judge ordered Wallace to stand down, forbidding him from interfering with the students' admission. President Kennedy hoped this injunction would prevent any planned violence on the day Hood and Malone enrolled in the University of Alabama, but he didn't want to take any chances.

On June 10, President Kennedy ordered National Guard troops to escort Malone and Hood to the university. As Hood and Malone approached the campus on the following day, Governor Wallace was waiting at the entrance to block their entry. Wallace was surrounded by state troopers and swarms of onlookers and media. The event, known as the "Stand in the Schoolhouse Door," was Wallace's attempt to keep his promise to the racists who had voted him into office. Despite giving an impassioned speech, the standoff ended with Wallace and his blockade stepping aside to allow the students inside.

Many elected local officials, like George Wallace (with his hand raised), refused to follow the law declaring segregated schools unconstitutional.

American writer James Baldwin (left) worked with Medgar Evers and other civil rights leaders to spotlight the treatment of African Americans in America.

An Off-the-Record Meeting

On May 24, 1963, Attorney General Robert F. Kennedy invited James Baldwin to his apartment in Manhattan to discuss race relations and the recent violence in Birmingham. James Baldwin was famous for honest depictions of Black America during the 1960s. In 1963, after traveling the world, Baldwin published *The Fire Next Time*, essays about race and religion that included a warning that violence would ensue if Black people were not given equality. Most at the meeting felt that Kennedy was ignorant of how widespread and damaging racism was in the United States. Baldwin left the meeting disappointed, feeling that the administration did not understand the urgency of the need for change.

The Aftermath

Vivian Malone would endure death threats and other acts of violence while living in campus dormitories. James Hood was harassed as well and withdrew from the university in August 1963. In November, three bombs were set off on campus, one of them just a few blocks from Malone's dorm room. Refusing to be intimidated, Malone continued on with her day. Some of the students on campus were nice to her, but she lived in relative isolation for the two years she attended the school. On May 30, 1965, Malone became the first African American student to graduate from the University of Alabama. ■

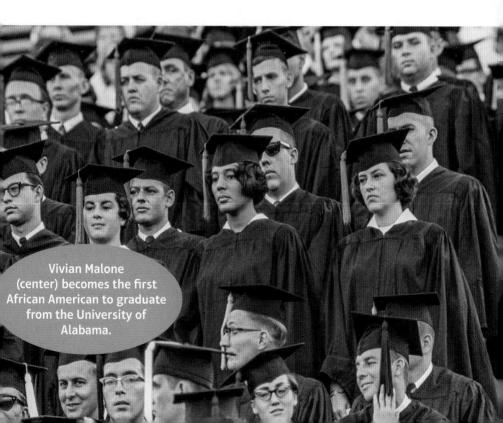

Vivian Malone (center) becomes the first African American to graduate from the University of Alabama.

Black demonstrators in Jackson, Mississippi, are arrested and carted to jail by the truckload for their involvement in a nonviolent protest.

4

A Summer of Strife

By June, images from the University of Alabama were on every television screen and in every newspaper in the United States. The success and momentum of the Birmingham Campaign shed light on civil rights issues in other states. Across the country, local civil rights movements used the traction to make gains in their own communities.

In most cases, these peaceful protesters were met with violence and resistance from govern-ment officials, local law enforcement, and white nationalist groups like the KKK. Racial tension and violence were at an all-time high as the summer of 1963 began.

Fearing the outbreak of violence against African Americans, President Kennedy addressed the nation on June 11, 1963. Kennedy's speech directly condemned segregation and racism against African Americans around the nation.

President Kennedy addresses the nation, asking all Americans to examine their conscience about the rights of Black citizens.

Kennedy said, "This Nation was founded by men of many nations and backgrounds. It was founded on the principle that all men are created equal, and that the rights of every man are diminished when the rights of one man are threatened." He spoke of the "fires of frustration . . . burning in every city" across the country. The historical call to action was one of the first times Kennedy had directly addressed the country about the treatment of Black Americans and was seen as a win for the movement. However, despite the cooling-off effect the speech was supposed to have, the country continued to burn.

The Assassination of Medgar Evers

On June 12, the day after President Kennedy's speech addressing the nation's civil rights struggles, activist Medgar Evers was assassinated by a member of the KKK in Jackson, Mississippi. Evers, who was working for the NAACP, had a long history of fighting for equality for Black Americans. Like many Black veterans of World War II, he found that life after the war had not granted him the rights given to white Americans. He was called to action after being denied the right to vote in a local election.

Evers was an outspoken leader in demanding justice for the death of Emmett Till, a young Black boy brutally murdered by two white men in 1955. That, as well as his ongoing success as a civil rights organizer, made him a target for racist white organizations like the KKK.

Civil rights leader Medgar Evers is laid to rest in Arlington National Cemetery in Arlington, Virginia.

Something in the Works

While the civil rights movement mourned the loss of Medgar Evers, a big idea began to take shape. In May, Dr. King and activist A. Philip Randolph developed a plan for a march on the nation's capital of Washington, DC. They both agreed that the march should be in August, as Congress would be in session during the month. King and Randolph appointed Bayard Rustin, a lead strategist for the Montgomery bus boycott, to oversee daily operations of the planned protest.

During the months of June and July, Rustin worked out of his office in Harlem, a Black section of New York City, organizing the details

On July 2, 1963, the "Big Six" civil rights leaders meet to formulate plans for the March on Washington. (From left to right: John Lewis, Whitney Young, Jr., Randolph, Dr. King, James Farmer, and Roy Wilkins)

Civil rights activist Bayard Rustin (right), the deputy director and chief organizer of the historic 1963 March on Washington, speaks to a group of volunteers.

of what would be known as the March on Washington for Jobs and Freedom. He recruited thousands of volunteers across the country and worked with Black organizations like the NAACP and CORE to build a team that eventually included organizations and religious groups like the National Catholic Conference for Interracial Justice and the American Jewish Congress.

Volunteers and organizers of the march were trained in the nonviolent methods of the movement. Many late nights and weekends were spent spreading information, coordinating transportation, and preparing meals for the anticipated 100,000 protesters.

A. Philip Randolph, president of the Brotherhood of Sleeping Car Porters and chair of the March on Washington, announces that more than the expected 100,000 people will participate.

A. Philip Randolph

A. Philip Randolph was one of the Big Six civil rights leaders. He had worked as a successful labor lawyer since the 1940s. Randolph was the head of the Brotherhood of Sleeping Car Porters, the first African American labor union. As a seasoned civil rights leader, Randolph knew there was strength in numbers. He had enlisted the help of other civil rights activists to work on the Birmingham Campaign. This would be Randolph's second time planning a march on Washington. The first march was designed to protest racism in the U.S. defense industry. That protest was called off when President Roosevelt signed an **Executive Order** (EO) in June 1941. EO 8802 prohibited discriminatory hiring practices by government agencies and businesses working on war-related projects.

The Mission of the March

The goal of the March on Washington was to advocate for a civil rights bill that was being held up in Congress. After years of protesting, activists were hopeful that the march would draw national attention and force Congress to pass the bill. Once the bill became law, civil rights activists hoped segregation in the country would end for good. The stalled legislation, known as the Civil Rights Act, called for the end of all segregated public spaces in the country and prohibited racial discrimination in the workplace, among other things.

Bayard Rustin (left) and Cleveland Robinson, chair of the Administrative Committee, meet to discuss the march.

A Private Meeting with Kennedy

On June 22, the Big Six civil rights leaders, including John Lewis, who led the Student Nonviolent Coordinating Committee (SNCC), met with President Kennedy at the White House. The men told the president about the planned march. The president did not support the idea. After the violent summer in the South, and with increased racial tension across the country, the president thought the march was "ill-timed." Kennedy tried to dissuade the men from marching at the capital, fearing the march would jeopardize the gains the movement had made and be used as another reason to further delay the Civil Rights Act. When the civil rights

On June 22, 1963, civil rights leaders meet Attorney General Robert Kennedy and other government officials at the White House.

Malcolm X speaks to reporters in Washington, DC, about his views on the civil rights movement.

leaders refused to back down, the president and his staff offered support in planning the day. He authorized the National Guard to be on standby in case there was violence, and the bars in Washington, DC, were all closed that day by law.

With the news of Kennedy's involvement, critics from both sides went on the attack. Some white citizens and government officials against the movement said the president should not interfere nor give aid. Black nationalist leaders such as Malcolm X also criticized the involvement of the U.S. government, which he did not trust. Malcolm X opposed Dr. King's nonviolent movement and felt Black Americans needed to create their own communities rather than look to white institutions for help. He and King represented two polarizing views within the fight for Black civil rights.

The March on Washington for Jobs and Freedom

On August 28, 1963, a quarter of a million people marched in Washington, DC, and peacefully gathered at the Lincoln Memorial in support of equal rights for Black Americans. Several celebrities were tasked with speaking, singing, and praying over the protesters. The Big Six civil rights leaders were welcomed to the mic, along with singer Mahalia Jackson and white organizers like Walter Reuther,

Overhead view of the massive crowd assembled during the March on Washington for Jobs and Freedom.

the president of the United Automobile Workers labor union. The excitement for the historic march on Washington had been building for months, as legal challenges against segregation in public institutions around the nation were successful. The massive turnout at the march exceeded the organizers' expectations. Black and white Americans unified to demand sweeping and permanent change. The joyful event was the largest civil rights demonstration in the nation's history and its impact on government and legislation in the months ahead was

Dr. King closed the day with his "I Have a Dream" speech.

> I have a dream that one day this nation will rise
> up and live out the true meaning of its creed:
> "We hold these truths to be self-evident, that all
> men are created equal."

The Women of the March

After the march, many of the male leaders of the march were invited to the White House to meet with the president. None of the women who helped organize the march were included in the invitation. Many of the successes that resulted from the March

Dorothy Height, head of the National Council of Negro Women and one of the organizers of the march, (right) listens as Dr. King addresses marchers with his "I Have a Dream" speech.

Singer and dancer Josephine Baker speaks on the steps of the Lincoln Memorial during the March on Washington.

on Washington, however, can be directly attributed to women organizers. Anna Arnold Hedgeman, a longtime activist, was the only woman on the planning committee. During the planning for the march, she pushed for female speakers but was outvoted by the men on the planning committee. Her angry response listing the contributions women had made to the movement over time helped change their minds.

Ultimately, women were featured in the program. Some female artists performed for the crowd, and a portion of the day's program was given to honoring "Negro Women Fighters for Freedom." Dorothy

Height, along with Rosa Parks, Daisy Bates, SNCC cofounder Diane Nash, and fearless activist Gloria Richardson, were applauded by the crowd along with the wives of the men of the movement.

Bates and Josephine Baker were the sole female voices to take the mic as speakers on the day of the march. Baker, who spoke before the official start of the program, talked about her time as an entertainer and how she used her voice to combat injustices, both in the entertainment industry and in the fight for civil rights.

Young women singing and clapping between speeches during the March on Washington.

Mahalia Jackson sings during the March on Washington. Sitting at lower right is Coretta Scott King with white-framed sunglasses.

Bates, who had successfully counseled and worked with the Little Rock Nine to integrate Central High School in Arkansas, was tasked with reading a short speech that had been prepared for her.

Coretta Scott King, Dr. King's wife, who in her own right had played a large part in planning the march, was also present. While the day undoubtedly marked a milestone for the movement, some women left feeling unappreciated. ∎

Black residents across the South were victims of house bombings by the KKK.

DANGER KEEP OUT

5

"Bombingham"

The peaceful March on Washington gave hope to many civil rights leaders and activists that real change was underway. But as fall approached, the nation's eye was, once again, focused on the South. This time, the battle to integrate all-white neighborhoods was ramping up across suburban neighborhoods, with particular focus on Birmingham.

Bombings of Black-owned homes in Birmingham had been going on since the late 1940s. The KKK used dynamite in a campaign of terror to keep Black families from integrating communities. By 1963, racial zoning ordinances made it almost impossible for Black residents to move beyond designated urban neighborhoods. Most of these inner-city neighborhoods enjoyed few or no amenities, had little access to quality health care or stores with healthy food options, and were run-down because landlords didn't see the need to update or maintain rental properties for Black residents. State-specific laws allowed local officials to keep residential areas segregated. This meant Black citizens could not buy homes in all-white neighborhoods, even if they could afford to.

Dynamite Hill

Intensifying the issue were the increased attacks on the few Black residents who had succeeded in integrating white neighborhoods like Center Street in North Smithfield, Birmingham. Over the span of 20 years leading up to 1963, more than 50 bombs were

Attorney Arthur Shores inspects bombing damage at his home in Birmingham, Alabama.

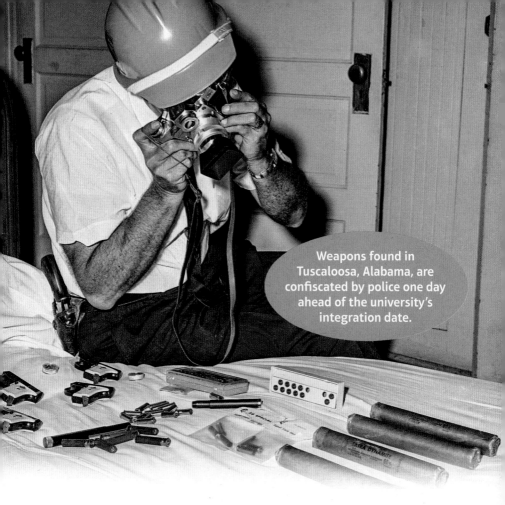

Weapons found in Tuscaloosa, Alabama, are confiscated by police one day ahead of the university's integration date.

detonated in the area. Most of the attacks were said to be the work of the KKK and other white nationalist groups. No one was prosecuted or arrested for any of the bombings.

Arthur Shores, a local attorney for the NAACP, had first challenged Birmingham's zoning laws in 1941. He had also helped with the court case that integrated the University of Alabama. His home, on the west side of Center Street, was one of only a handful of houses owned by Black families on a mostly white block. As a result of his continuing work for the NAACP, the

Art Capturing the Civil Rights Movement

Mississippi Freedom Marcher, Washington D.C., 1963, a photograph by Roy DeCarava.

Increased awareness within the civil rights movement helped to spotlight art by African American artists. In 1963, a group of 15 notable artists who were also activists founded the Spiral Group. They wanted to create and showcase art that spoke about the struggles Black people experienced fighting for equality. Much of the Spiral Group's work received critical acclaim, including photographer Roy DeCarava's image *Mississippi Freedom Marcher, Washington, D.C., 1963*. The photograph was taken at the March on Washington and would become one of the many pieces of art capturing the movement.

windows of his home were frequently shot out and his family survived two different bombings. Shores's children were unable to even walk through their town for fear of attack.

Over the years, North Smithfield came to be known to locals as Dynamite Hill. During 1963, several Black youth and adult activists would lose their lives as a result of these bombings. ■

State troopers stand guard with city police at Graymont Elementary School in the North Smithfield community of Birmingham, Alabama, after it was integrated.

On September 15, a bomb ripped through the 16th Street Baptist Church in Birmingham.

6

The 16th Street Church Bombing

Since the start of the civil rights movement, the 16th Street Baptist Church in Birmingham had been a safe haven for civil rights activists and supporters. As a cornerstone of the movement, the church served as a central meeting spot for strategy sessions, protests, and rallies. Because of this role, the church was targeted by opposition groups like the KKK, who wanted to intimidate and hinder the movement.

On Sunday morning, September 15, church-goers gathered for worship services. On this day, however, members of the KKK had hidden 19 sticks of dynamite under the east side of the building. At 10 a.m., Sunday School children and teenagers entered the building. Adult members of the church gathered in the front, to await the start of morning service at 11 a.m.

Police and firefighters investigate the large crater left by the bomb that exploded in the basement of the 16th Street Baptist Church in Birmingham.

At 10:22 a.m., an unidentified caller rang the Sunday School secretary's phone line at the church and left the coded message "Three minutes" before hanging up. Rigged to a timer, the bomb exploded within the next minute, destroying the basement of the church where five young girls were getting ready for services. The powerful blast tore through the building walls, injuring people inside, outside, and one man driving by in his car.

Unspeakable Tragedy

Church members and Black citizens across the city immediately sprang into action, sorting through the debris for survivors. When the dust settled, four of the young girls were dead. Their bodies were recovered in the rubble. The fifth girl in the room with them was severely injured and ended up losing her eye.

Within hours of the blast, hundreds of outraged citizens took to the streets, marching downtown to demand justice. As in the riots earlier that year, businesses and buildings were torched and destroyed. Black and white residents threw bottles, bricks, and other debris at one another and fights broke out in the street.

The family of one of the four African American girls killed in the 16th Street Baptist Church bombing.

Governor Wallace deployed more than 300 additional police troops into the area. These measures only managed to make things worse. The unrest within the city took hours to control, lasting until early next morning. When it was over, two Black teenage boys had been shot and killed by police officers.

On September 16, President Kennedy addressed the nation again, this time about the bombings in Birmingham. In his speech he expressed a "deep sense of outrage and grief over the killing of the children yesterday in Birmingham, Alabama."

The Fight for Justice

Immediately after the bombings, Dr. King sent a telegram to the governor of Alabama stating that "the blood of our little children is on your hands." Once again, the fight for Black civil rights was center stage in national and international media. Civil rights leaders did not trust local officials to properly investigate the bombings. They felt more confident when the FBI became involved.

The FBI investigation into the church bombing was swift, but justice would be slow. The initial investigation identified four KKK members as suspects, but making charges stick would be an uphill battle.

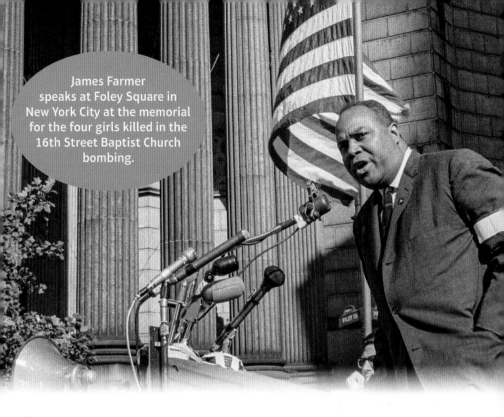

James Farmer speaks at Foley Square in New York City at the memorial for the four girls killed in the 16th Street Baptist Church bombing.

In 1965, Robert Chambliss, Bobby Frank Cherry, Herman Cash, and Thomas Blanton were questioned about their involvement in the bombing. The FBI invited anyone else with information about the bombing to come forward, but no one did. Without more evidence or witnesses, no charges could be proved. The case went cold. In 1971, the case was reopened and six years later one bomber, Robert Chambliss, was convicted of murder. Herman Cash died in 1994 without being convicted, and it would take several more years for the last two bombers to be convicted. Thomas Blanton was convicted in 2001, 24 years after Chambliss, and Bobby Frank Cherry was convicted in 2002.

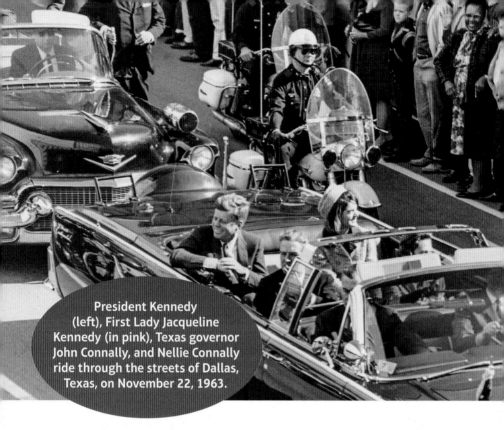

President Kennedy (left), First Lady Jacqueline Kennedy (in pink), Texas governor John Connally, and Nellie Connally ride through the streets of Dallas, Texas, on November 22, 1963.

Assassination of President Kennedy

Toward the end of a very violent year in the fight for civil rights, President Kennedy was assassinated. On November 22, he and Mrs. Kennedy, along with the governor of Texas and his wife, were traveling in a motorcade in Dallas, Texas. Lee Harvey Oswald's bullet killed Kennedy and seriously wounded Governor Connally. After the President's death, Vice President Lyndon B. Johnson was sworn into office. While there was never a direct link between the assassination and the civil rights movement, many supporters of the movement believed that Kennedy's championship may have been one driving force in his killing.

The Presidential Medal of Freedom

The Presidential Medal of Freedom is awarded for contributions to the national interests of the United States, world peace, or cultural endeavors. Dr. Ralph Bunche became the first African American to be awarded the Presidential Medal of Freedom, created by President Kennedy in 1963. Bunche was a diplomat in the State Department who had also been the first African American to receive the Nobel Peace Prize. Opera singer Marian Anderson also received the award in 1963.

Nobel Prize–winning political scientist and diplomat Ralph Bunche (1904–1971).

The Movement Presses Forward

Spurred by tragic events in Birmingham, civil rights protests were happening across the country by the end of the year. On October 22, a school boycott was planned for all the public schools in Chicago, Illinois.

In the years leading up to 1963, schools in Chicago were severely segregated. Wealthy school boards in whites-only districts found ways to avoid integration. This led to overcrowding and declining conditions in Black inner-city schools.

Educational activists called for Black students to attend whites-only schools. They wanted students who could not walk to these schools to be bussed to them, and they wanted to stop the city from allowing more money to be funneled into whites-only public school districts.

On October 22, more than 200,000 students were absent from Chicago's schools and another 10,000 rallied outside the board of education office. Protesters who were advocating for better educational conditions for Black students wanted their voices to be heard.

The boycott didn't result in many changes for Black students in Chicago, but it did shine a spotlight on the differences between white and Black students' access to quality education in the city. ∎

International Fight for Black Civil Rights

Like African Americans in the United States, Black citizens across the world were also fighting for civil rights and independence. On December 12, the African nation of Kenya declared its independence from Britain. The victory marked an end to the colonial reign over the country and turned its resources and governmental power over to the Kenyan people.

Jomo Kenyatta, the first president of an independent Kenya.

Marching crowds hold signs during the March on Washington for Jobs and Freedom.

The Legacy of 1963 in Civil Rights History

As 1963 began, civil rights activists had focused their attention on the South. With a series of planned, targeted campaigns, the movement began to see gains in equal rights for African Americans.

In Birmingham, "Whites-Only" and "Blacks-Only" signs were removed from businesses, and some public schools and universities admitted Black students. Segregated facilities were outlawed and most public spaces were integrated.

Yet in the South, particularly, local government officials continued to resist change. Many relied on states' rights to dismiss federal law and continued to mistreat Black residents. However, the federal government's support in enforcing the laws of the land gave hope to leaders. When 250,000 civil rights activists joined the March on Washington in August, the nation listened as Dr. King spoke of his dream for a society where men and women of color had the same opportunities as white people.

On November 22, Lyndon B. Johnson was sworn in as the president of the United States. He would continue President Kennedy's work alongside civil rights leaders.

By 1964, the mission of leaders like King, Dorothy Height, John Lewis, and others who had pressed for equal voting rights for Black Americans paid off. In January 1964, Congress passed the Twenty-Fourth Amendment to the Constitution, banning direct attempts to suppress Black voters. This amendment applied only to national elections, but it would pave the way for a broader success in 1966. The Supreme Court decision *Harper v. Virginia State Board of Elections* declared that Virginia's poll tax was a violation of the Fourteenth Amendment's equal protection clause. As a result, poll taxes around the country would be discontinued for both national and local elections.

Dr. King meets with President Johnson during a visit to the White House in December 1963.

Lyndon Johnson signs the Civil Rights Act on July 2, 1964.

The Civil Rights Act Passes

A major victory that resulted from the events of 1963 was the passing of the Civil Rights Act of 1964. On July 2, after months in Congress, the bill was passed into law. On the day President Johnson signed the bill, he was surrounded by members of Congress and several civil rights leaders. The Civil Rights Act of 1964 marked a major milestone in the long-fought war against the discriminatory practices against Black Americans in the United States. Even with the gains from 1963, however, the fight for equal civil rights for African Americans would continue for years to come. ■

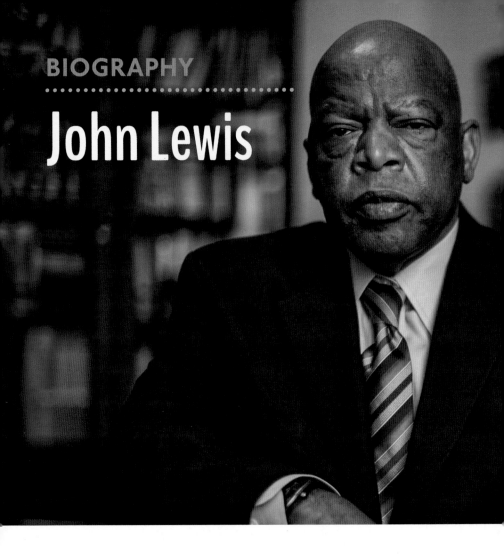

John Lewis

John Lewis, known to many as one of the Big Six, was devoted to securing voting rights for African Americans.

Lewis was born on February 21, 1940, in Troy, Alabama. His parents were share-croppers who taught him that hard work brings success. At a young age Lewis was very aware of the injustices facing African Americans in the United States. At the age of 11 he traveled to visit family in the Nort and saw firsthand how differently African Americans were treated in the North, compared to his home in the South.

Congressman John Lewis was one of the Big Six leaders of the civil rights movement.

Growing up, Lewis wanted to be a preacher and admired the work that Dr. King was doing across the country. He followed the Montgomery bus boycott closely and studied King's speeches. As a teenager, Lewis met Rosa Parks and King. He was moved and inspired by both activists and planned to follow in their footsteps.

Lewis became a student activist in Nashville. He attended the American Baptist Theological Seminary, where he studied religion and philosophy.

In 1961, Lewis was one of the organizers of the **Freedom Riders** and was repeatedly

John Lewis poses in his Atlanta office with two of his favorite items from his collection of civil rights memorabilia.

arrested for trying to integrate northern interstate transportation systems. In 1963, he became the head of the Student Nonviolent Coordinating Committee (SNCC). After aiding in the Birmingham Campaign and the March on Washington for Jobs and Freedom, Lewis focused his attention on equal voting rights for Black people.

Lewis helped organize another historical march from Selma to Montgomery, Alabama,

"If not us, then who? If not now, then when?"
—JOHN LEWIS

John Lewis, second from left, in 1965.

with Hosea Williams, a close friend of King's. The five-day protest was planned to shed light on unfair voting practices aimed at African American citizens. On March 7, 1965, Lewis and more than 600 peaceful protesters, marching across the Edmund Pettus Bridge in Selma, were brutally attacked and beaten on orders from Alabama's governor, George Wallace.

President Barack Obama awards the Medal of Freedom to Lewis on February 15, 2011.

Lewis left SNCC in 1966 to complete his schooling, but continued to fight for equal rights with organizations like the Voter Education Project, which added nearly four million minority citizens to the voting rolls while he was director. In 1986, John Lewis was elected to the U.S. House of Representatives from Georgia. Lewis's lifelong crusade for rights for poor and disenfranchised people earned him the nickname "the conscience of the Congress." He continued to protest and march for causes throughout his life, and even held a sit-in on the floor of the House of Representatives in 2016 to protest the lack of action by the government on gun violence. At his funeral in 2020, Speaker of the House Nancy Pelosi and former presidents Clinton, Bush, and Obama all spoke of his courage, kindness, and relentless pursuit of equality for all.

TIMELINE

The Year in Civil Rights

1963

JANUARY 14

George Wallace takes his oath of office as governor of Alabama, vowing to uphold segregation forever.

APRIL 3

The Birmingham Campaign launches with a march to city hall.

APRIL 16

While in jail, King starts writing Letter from Birmingham Jail, which makes national news and draws attention to racial inequalities in the South.

MAY 2

The Children's Crusade launches. Several school-age students (as young as seven years old) are arrested and released the same day.

MAY 3

On the second day of the peaceful Children's Crusade, students are attacked by police dogs and officers wielding fire hoses.

MAY 10

After a week of protest and media coverage, business owners in Birmingham call for a truce and sign the Birmingham Agreement with civil rights leaders.

MAY 11

The home of A. D. King and the hotel where Dr. King is staying are bombed.

MAY 16

The NAACP wins a big victory with the integration of the University of Alabama. The school is required to admit its first Black students.

JUNE 11

Governor George Wallace blocks entry into the University of Alabama in the "Stand in the School-house Door." However, National Guards are deployed and two Black students are enrolled.

AUGUST 28

The March on Washington for Jobs and Freedom takes place in Washington, DC. King delivers his famous "I Have a Dream" speech.

SEPTEMBER 15

The 16th Street Baptist Church is bombed. Four young girls are killed in the explosion.

SEPTEMBER 16

President Kennedy calls for an end to the violence targeted against the civil rights movement across the nation.

NOVEMBER 22

President Kennedy is assassinated.

GLOSSARY

activist (AK-tiv-ist) a person who works to bring about political or social change

amenities (uh-MEN-i-tees) desirable or useful features of a building or place

boycott (BOI-kaht) a refusal to buy something or do business with someone as a protest

contempt of court (kuhn-TEMPT ohv kort) the offense of being disobedient or disrespectful of a court of law and its officers

civil rights (SIV-uhl rites) the individual rights that all members of a democratic society have, such as freedom and equal treatment under the law

descendants (di-SEN-duhnts) your children, their children, and so on into the future

desegregate (dee-SEG-ruh-gayt) to do away with the practice of separating people of different races in schools, restaurants, and other public places

discrimination (dis-krim-uh-NAY-shuhn) prejudice or unfair behavior to others based on differences in such things as race, gender, or age

endanger (en-DAYN-jur) to put in peril; to threaten

executive order (egg-ZEC-yuh-tiv OR-dur) a rule or order issued by the president to an executive branch of government and having the force of law

federal (FED-ur-uhl) national government, as opposed to local or state government

Freedom Rider (FREE-dum RYE-dur) a person who challenged racial laws in the American South in the 1960s by refusing to follow the segregation laws on buses

injunction (in-JUNK-shuhn) a warning or order given by an authority

integration (IN-tuh-gray-shuhn) the practice of uniting people from different races in an attempt to give people equal rights

Jim Crow (jim kro) the former practice of segregating Black people in the United States.

Ku Klux Klan (KOO klux KLAN) a secret organization in the United States that uses threats and violence to achieve its goal of white supremacy; also called the Klan or the KKK

lawsuit (LAW-soot) a legal action or case brought against a person or group in a court of law

literacy (LIT-ur-uh-see) the ability to read and write

lynching (LIN-ching) a sometimes public murder by a group of people, often involving hanging

moderate (MAH-dur-it) less severe or extreme

oppression (uh-PRESH-uhn) the act of treating people in a cruel and unjust way

ordinance (OR-duh-nuhnts) an authoritative order; a decree

poll tax (pohl taks) a tax of a fixed amount per person placed on adults and often linked to the right to vote

scrutiny (SCREW-tin-ee) close examination or study

segregation (seg-ruh-GAY-shuhn) the act or practice of keeping people or groups apart

sit-in (SIT-in) a form of protest in which demonstrators occupy a place, refusing to leave until their demands are met

truce (troos) an agreement between enemies to stop fighting for a short time

unconstitutional (uhn-kahn-stuh-TOO-shuh-nuhl) something that is forbidden by the Constitution

volatile (VAH-luh-tuhl) showing a rapid change of mood, usually instability

zoning (ZOHN-ing) laws that separate areas of a community for special purposes

BIBLIOGRAPHY

Bernstein, A. "James Hood, Who Integrated University of Alabama, Dies at 70." *Washington Post*, January 18, 2013. washingtonpost.com/local/obituaries/james-hood-who-integrated-university-of-alabama-dies-at-70/2013/01/18/c990b724-6198-11e2-9940-6fc488f3fecd_story.html

Civil Rights Act. (n.d.). britannica.com/event/Civil-Rights-Act-United-States-1964

Clark-Robinson, M., F. Morrison, and J. Edwards. *Let the Children March*. Solon, OH: Findaway World, 2019.

Elliott, D. "Remembering Birmingham's 'Dynamite Hill' Neighborhood." NPR, July 6, 2013. npr.org/sections/codeswitch/2013/07/06/197342590/remembering-birminghams-dynamite-hill-neighborhood

Gaboury, F. "Eight Days in May: Birmingham and the Struggle for Civil Rights." May 4, 2017. peoplesworld.org/article/eight-days-in-may-birmingham-and-the-struggle-for-civil-rights/

HISTORY at Home: Lessons and Activities.com. (n.d.). history.com/history-at-home-activities

Kennedy, John F. Televised Address to the Nation on Civil Rights. (n.d.). jfklibrary.org/learn/about-jfk/historic-speeches/televised-address-to-the-nation-on-civil-rights

Levinson, C. *We've Got a Job: The 1963 Birmingham Children's March*. Atlanta, GA: Peachtree, 2014.

March on Washington for Jobs and Freedom, 1963. kinginstitute.stanford.edu/encyclopedia/march-washington-jobs-and-freedom

Palmer, M. "Woolworth's Sit-In." July 27, 2018. civilrightsteaching.org/1963/woolworths-sit-in

Smith, K. "Remembering Daisy Bates: Orator at the March on Washington." (n.d.) facingtoday.facinghistory.org/celebrating-daisy-bates-black-female-orator-at-the-march-on-washington

Sugrue, T. J. *Sweet Land of Liberty: The Forgotten Struggle for Civil Rights in the North*. New York: Random House, 2009.

Summer of 1963. August 26, 2013. americanhistory.si.edu/changing-america-emancipation-procla-mation-1863-and-march-washington-1963/1963/summer-1963-0

Taylor, A. "50 Years Ago: The World in 1963." February 15, 2013. theatlantic.com/photo/2013/02/50-years-ago-the-world-in-1963/100460/?utm_source=twitter&utm_medium=so-cial&utm_campaign=share

U.S. National Park Service. (n.d.). nps.gov/

Washington Post. (n.d.) washingtonpost.com/wp-srv/politics/daily/sept98/wallace.htm

INDEX

About the Author

Angela Shanté is the award-winning author of *The Noisy Classroom*, a picture book about her time as a classroom teacher. She grew up in New York City where she first fell in love with words and teaching. Angela received a Master's in Elementary Education with a focus on literacy and later went back to school to receive an MFA in Creative Writing. With one leg in education and the other in the creative world, Angela marries her two passions by creating creative content for young readers across all mediums. Angela currently lives in Southern California with her husband and dog (Blue).

PHOTO CREDITS

The years from 1955 to 1965 are at the heart of the civil rights movement. Resistance was often met with violence against Black Americans struggling to end discrimination and segregation. Yet the courage of those yearning for equal opportunities under the law continued to persevere.

The year 1963 was memorable for both the violence against Black Americans and the words and actions it inspired. In June, two Black students were blocked from registering for classes at the University of Alabama. Civil rights leaders responded with a historic protest. In August, 250,000 people gathered for the March on Washington as Dr. Martin Luther King, Jr., delivered his "I Have a Dream" speech. The following month, a bomb planted by the Ku Klux Klan killed four girls at a church in Birmingham. As the extent of racism and discrimination became more apparent, support for the movement swelled and change now seemed inevitable.

This detailed account explains why 1963 was such a critical year in the civil rights movement.

ALSO AVAILABLE

Franklin Watts® an imprint of

SCHOLASTIC

scholastic.com/library publishing

$11.99 US
$15.99 CAN

ISBN 978-1-338-76981-4

9 781338 769814